D1309726

CRAFT IT!

Valentine's Day

Gifts

Anastasia Suen

Rourke
Educational Media

rourkeeducationalmedia.com

TABLE OF CONTENTS

MATERIALS NEEDED FOR ALL PROJECTS

- air-dry clay
- bag of candy hearts
- buttons
- chalk
- clear tape or rubber bands
- cookie cutter hearts
- felt
- foam board
- glue or **decoupage**
- miniature canvas and easel
- needle
- newspaper or cloth to cover your work area
- paint
- paintbrush or foam brush
- paper
- paper plate
- pencil
- picture frame
- plastic straw
- poster paper
- ribbon, cord, or yarn
- rolling pin
- scissors
- scratch paper
- straight pins
- thumbtacks
- toilet paper rolls
- yarn, string, or embroidery floss

VALENTINE'S DAY GIFTS

Valentine's Day is coming! Show your love with a handmade gift. Paint a hearts poster. Create a mini **masterpiece** or a candy hearts frame. Decorate clay heart **charms**. Sew tiny felt Valentine's envelopes. Make a heart with string.

These handmade Valentine's gifts can be enjoyed year-round.

Make a heart stamp poster.

Here's How:

1. Fold an empty toilet paper roll in half.
2. Press the top of the roll down. Form a heart shape.
3. Use tape or rubber bands around the ends to hold the heart shape.

You Will Need:
- newspaper or cloth to cover your work area
- empty toilet paper rolls
- clear tape or rubber bands
- paint
- small paper plate for each paint color
- poster paper
- picture frame

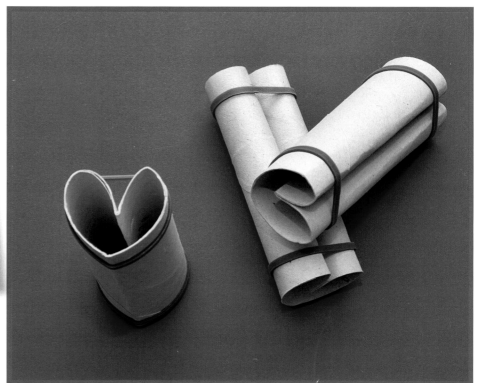

4. Make a new heart stamp for each color.
5. Pour paint onto a paper plate. Make a stamp pad for each color.
6. Dip a stamp into the paint.
7. Press the stamp on the poster. Cover the poster with hearts.
8. Add more paint to the stamp as needed.

9. Repeat with the next color. Cover the poster with colorful hearts.

10. After the paint dries, frame the poster.

Heart Stamp Wrapping Paper:
You can also make heart stamp wrapping paper. Stamp colorful hearts on large sheets of thin paper or tissue paper. Use your handmade wrapping paper for the gifts you make in this book!

TIP!
Add each new color on top of the others. When the hearts overlap it creates the **illusion** of depth.

Decorate a picture frame with candy hearts.

Here's How:

1. Remove the glass, paper, and cardboard from the picture frame.
2. Paint the frame.

You Will Need:
- newspaper or cloth to cover your work area
- picture frame
- acrylic paint
- paintbrush
- bag of candy hearts
- glue

TIP!
You can paint a new unfinished wood frame or re-use an old picture frame.

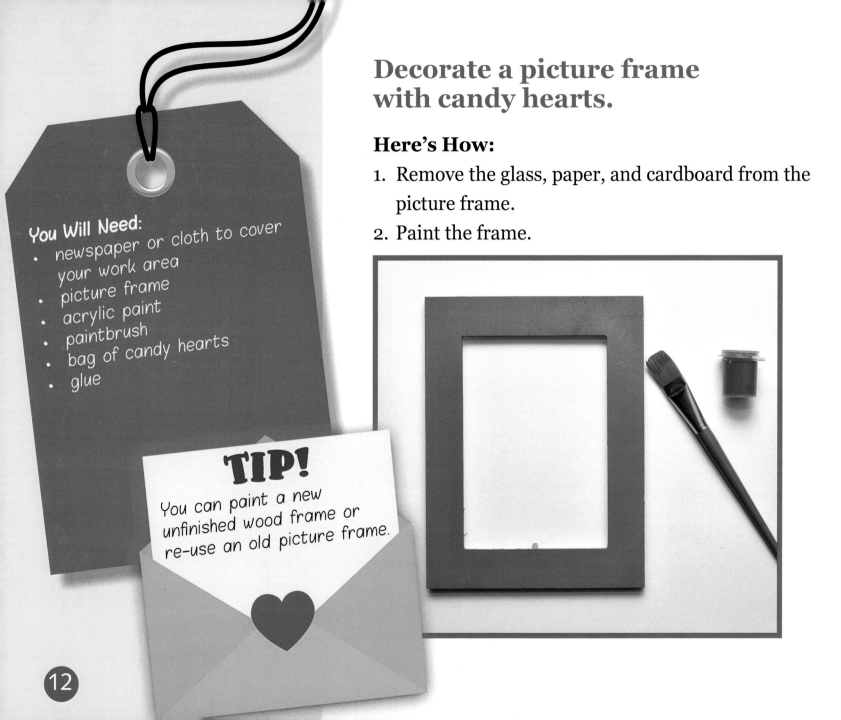

3. Let the paint dry overnight.
4. Glue candy hearts in a row around the frame. Add a drop of glue. Place a candy heart on the glue. Gently hold it as you count to ten. Repeat.
5. Let the glue dry overnight.

6. Put the glass back into the frame. Add a picture.

TIP!
Be sure to keep your fingers dry. If the candy hearts get wet, the words will disappear.

All Candy:

You can also cover the entire frame with candy. Glue a single row of candy around a thin frame, or use multiple rows of candy for a wider frame.

Make a mini masterpiece! This gift can be enjoyed year round.

Here's How:

1. Fold colorful paper in half. Cut a small heart shape.
2. Repeat three times. Use different paper for each heart.

You Will Need:
- newspaper or cloth to cover your work area
- miniature canvas and **easel**
- scissors
- colorful paper (in four different patterns)
- scratch paper
- decoupage or glue
- paintbrush or foam brush

TIP!

Use scratch paper to test the best size for your paper hearts.

3. Place a small paper heart in each corner of the canvas.
4. Lift one heart. Brush glue on the back.
5. Place it on the tiny canvas.
6. Use your finger to smooth out any bubbles.

7. One by one, glue the other hearts.
8. Brush the entire canvas with glue to seal it.

TIP!
Move the hearts into a design you like before you add the glue.

9. Place canvas on the easel to display.

Spell Love:

Spell the word LOVE with tiny letters. You can also paint or stencil the letters on the canvas with acrylic paint.

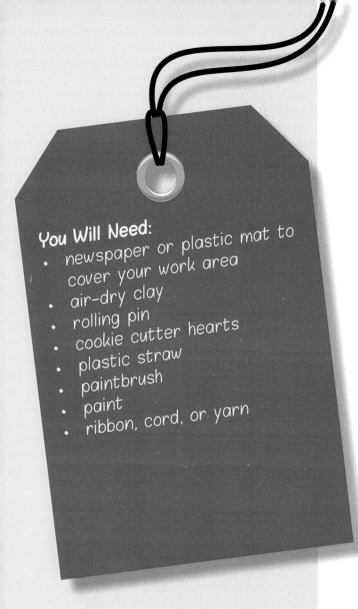

You Will Need:
- newspaper or plastic mat to cover your work area
- air-dry clay
- rolling pin
- cookie cutter hearts
- plastic straw
- paintbrush
- paint
- ribbon, cord, or yarn

Make a clay heart charm.

Here's How:

1. Roll the ball of clay on a clean surface.
2. Use a rolling pin to make the clay one quarter inch (6 millimeters) thick.

TIP!
Roll the clay in your hands first to warm it up.

3. Press the cookie cutter into the clay to make heart shapes.

4. Poke a hole in the center at the top. Use a plastic straw.
5. Let the clay dry overnight.

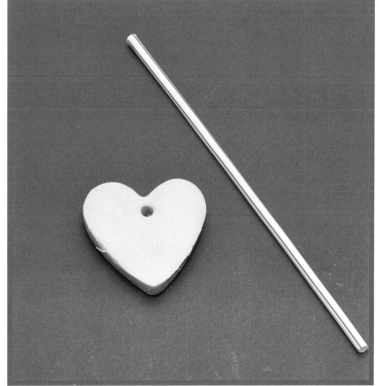

6. Paint a colorful **border**. Go around the edge of each heart.

7. After the paint dries, pull a ribbon or cord through the hole. Tie a knot.

TIP!

To make a border, choose a shape that you can repeat all around the edge.

"You and Me" Charms

If you cut out hearts in different sizes, you can make "you and me" charms. For these charms, make a hole on the upper right side of each heart. After the hearts dry, paint them differen colors. When the paint dries, place the small heart on top of the big heart. Pull a ribbon or cord through both hearts and tie a knot.

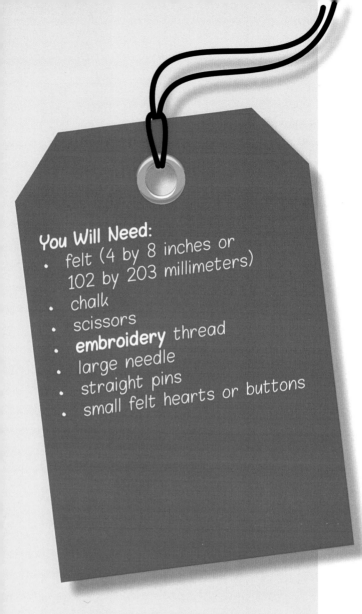

You Will Need:
- felt (4 by 8 inches or 102 by 203 millimeters)
- chalk
- scissors
- **embroidery** thread
- large needle
- straight pins
- small felt hearts or buttons

Make tiny felt envelopes.

Here's How:

1. Fold the felt in half the long way.
2. On the outer edge, measure 1.5 inches (3.8 centimeters) from the top. Make a dot with chalk.
3. Place the ruler across the top of the folded felt. Draw a line from the dot to the other corner.

4. Lift up the ruler and cut on the line. Keep the felt folded when you cut.
5. Unfold the felt.

6. Cut 18 inches (46 centimeters) of embroidery thread.
7. Thread the needle. Tie a single knot.

TIP!
If you keep the felt folded when you cut, the felt will look the same on both sides.

How to tie a single knot:

Pull the thread through the needle until both ends meet.

Make a loop with the ends.

Pull the ends through the loop.

Pull into a knot.

8. Fold the bottom up. Pin the sides together.

9. Begin sewing at the top of the triangle. Make short straight stitches. Sew down one side of the triangle.

10. Sew the body of the envelope. Sew all three sides.

11. Sew up the other side of the flap.

12. Sew or glue a small heart on the top of the triangle.

TIP!
Use straight pins to hold the felt together while you sew.

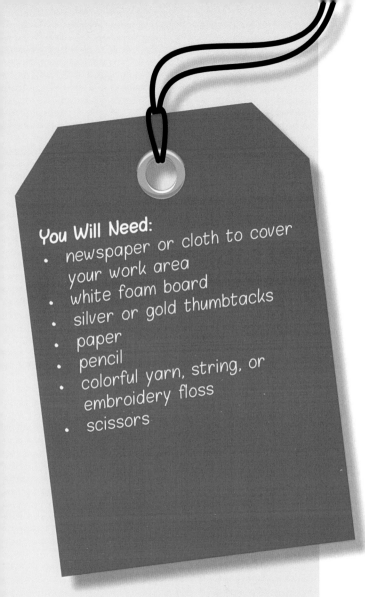

You Will Need:
- newspaper or cloth to cover your work area
- white foam board
- silver or gold thumbtacks
- paper
- pencil
- colorful yarn, string, or embroidery floss
- scissors

String a Heart

Here's How:

1. Fold a sheet of paper in half. Cut a heart shape.

2. Place the paper heart on the foam board.
3. Push thumbtacks around the edge of the heart.
4. Remove the paper heart.

6. Pull the string to a new thumbtack. Wrap the string around it.
7. Repeat until you fill the heart.
8. Tie a knot around the last thumbtack. Cut the end of the string.
9. Press the thumbtacks all the way down.

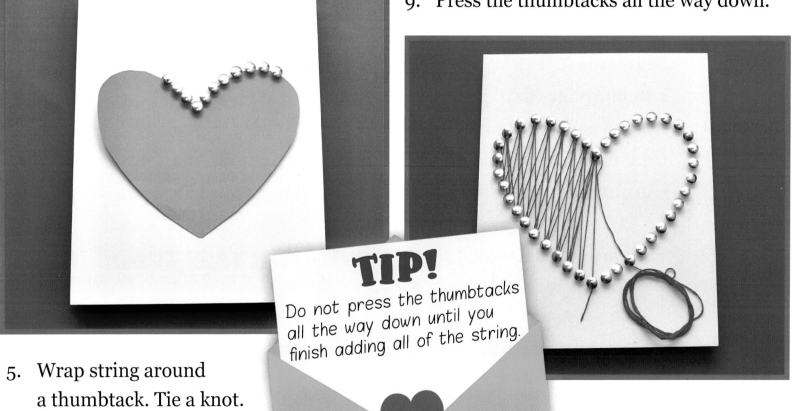

5. Wrap string around a thumbtack. Tie a knot.

TIP!
Do not press the thumbtacks all the way down until you finish adding all of the string.

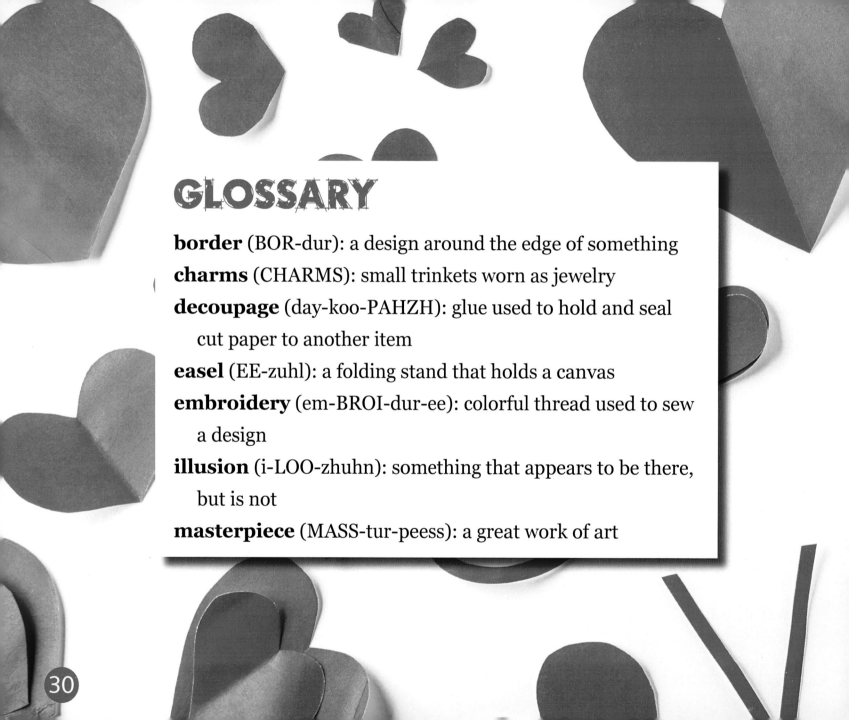

GLOSSARY

border (BOR-dur): a design around the edge of something

charms (CHARMS): small trinkets worn as jewelry

decoupage (day-koo-PAHZH): glue used to hold and seal cut paper to another item

easel (EE-zuhl): a folding stand that holds a canvas

embroidery (em-BROI-dur-ee): colorful thread used to sew a design

illusion (i-LOO-zhuhn): something that appears to be there, but is not

masterpiece (MASS-tur-peess): a great work of art

INDEX

SHOW WHAT YOU KNOW

1. How did you make the paper roll stay in a heart shape?

2. Describe how you can create the illusion of depth.

3. Explain why each heart is glued twice to make a mini masterpiece.

4. Describe how to make a hole in a clay charm.

5. How can you finish the flap of the felt envelope?

WEBSITES TO VISIT

www.woohome.com/diy-2/30-fun-and-easy-diy-valentines-day-crafts-kids-can-make

www.ducksters.com/holidays/valentines_day.php

www.wikihow.com/Thread-a-Needle-and-Tie-a-Knot

ABOUT THE AUTHOR

As a child, Anastasia Suen made and wrapped Valentine's Day gifts at the kitchen table. Today she uses that same kitchen table to make and wrap Valentine's Day gifts in her studio in Northern California.

Meet The Author!
www.meetREMauthors.com

© 2018 Rourke Educational Media

All rights reserved. No part of this book may be reproduced or utilized in any form or by any means, electronic or mechanical including photocopying, recording, or by any information storage and retrieval system without permission in writing from the publisher.

www.rourkeeducationalmedia.com

PHOTO CREDITS: All photos © Blue Door Publishing, FL. except the following from Shutterstock.com: Page 4-5 © OnlyZoia; page 6 © Mariia Boiko; Tip icon throughout © Melody ; page 7 © Stephen Coburn; page 11 background photo without candy heart frame and background photo page 15 © Photographee.eu, photo inside frame © hotbox; page 30 © Olga Larionova

Edited by: Keli Sipperley

Cover and Interior design by: Nicola Stratford   www.nicolastratford.com
Thank you, Ashley Hayasaka, for making the crafts.

Library of Congress PCN Data

Valentine's Day Gifts / Anastasia Suen
(Craft It!)
 ISBN 978-1-68342-374-4 (hard cover)
 ISBN 978-1-68342-883-1 (soft cover)
 ISBN 978-1-68342-540-3 (e-Book)
Library of Congress Control Number: 2017931274

Rourke Educational Media
Printed in the United States of America, North Manchester, Indiana

FREDERICK COUNTY PUBLIC LIBRARIES

NOV   2018